Ode to Every Little Thing

Siera Zamarron

Presentation by *BookLeaf Publishing*

Web: www.bookleafpub.com

E-mail: info@bookleafpub.com

ISBN: 9789358367928

First edition 2024

My siblings and my mother,

My best friend Alissa,

my cat Yuki,

and the dearest person to me in my life, Jonah

ACKNOWLEDGEMENT

Special thanks to my closest friends for their unwavering support, my best friend Alissa for being my rock during the hardest times of my life, the Schmuker family for reminding me what home feels like and Jonah for loving me as I am and making life truly feel like an adventure.

PREFACE

These are little stories, little snippets and bits and pieces of my life, feelings, who I am, who those in my life are to me, the beautiful moments, the angry ones, the ever so dreadful ones. Just, a tad bit of everything, stuffed and compiled into this book here. I pour every quivering bit of my soul into each loving, somber, joyous, and angry paragraph. This is it. This is me. I hope you'll find a piece of yourself within these pages. I found more of myself writing them than I could have ever imagined...

martyr

you sought
to tear
me
down
with every
grueling,
verbose blow
...
you never
expected
me to
come back
building myself
upon a tower
higher than ever
your derelict
trebuchet
could never dare
to reach
me

always never

you are always never
plagued by always
tripping on never

i will never understand
whatever you say?
whatever you do?
never satisfied
always drenched in dismay
whenever
always and forever
it's never you
but it's always us
however
no matter what is done
wherever and by whoever
it lies static in your mind
whatsoever
it's no longer worth
the endeavor

i give up
you are always never

good bye

nothing aches more
than letting you go
i have to
(i'm sorry)
otherwise
i will end up
letting myself go

It's Been The Rest of My Life, How's the Weather?

I watched you plant
Those flowers
And I saw them wither
At your feet

You tried watering, and cutting
Away at the weeds
Thorns pricked at your thumbs
And you bleed
And bleed
And bled

Flowers bloom
At this time of year
Haven't seen you in a long time
Did you plant a new garden
Is the weather nice up there?

compass

the needle
drawn
drawing you away

the needle
pointing
that led you astray

pane

looking behind me
those glass window pane memories
who we were before suddenly
why they're all stained red

time and time again
i never realized missing you
would be something i both
crave and dread

rain's lullaby

at least
even when
this house isn't a home
the pitter patter
of raindrops
will drown out
my sorrows
my doubts
mind's mindless chatter

and maybe
i can fall asleep
to its song
and wake up
to morning dew
and energy
and strength
to begin anew

it ends with me

i am sorry
for what
your father's father
did to his sons

i am sorry
that your mother's burdens
have spread
infected everyone

and
i'm sorry
that this genetic distress
caused you to turn into
all that you've become

and
i'm sorry
but it ends with me
i won't turn into them
i will not become one

rot not naught

the subtlety of the lamented dove
splayed hugging the soil
her new home in the earth
born a flora refuge

the fallen fruit
which does not just perish
but for the creatures who are pygmy
bares a lavish banquet

with the gentle clicking
the turning gears of a clock
even that
which turns to rot
refuses to be
all for naught

Alissa

her smile is radiant
reminiscent of daylight
she'll be ever mirthful
when you stumble
onto the floor

yet
she's ever the first
to lift you up
off the ground
she listens kindly
with an open heart

yet
unabashedly calls you out
on your foolishness

When
the room is dark
she'll hold up a match
burn her fingertips
just so you can see

dearest
to me

lucky am I
to have she

this poem tastes like wisdom

12

why
does
tragedy
garnish
boring regular reality

why
does
the ugly
make
the beautiful
taste
so much better

keep going

the creek still babbles on
robins still whistle their songs
trees still wave hello
when all seems to have gone wrong

stars still dot the skies
crickets chirp lamented lullabies
mothers coo while babies cry
despite life's turns seeming awry

home

there's something warm
about them
when they open up the door
when they smile
those smiles that i can't help
but adore

gentle fire crackling
laughter, that roar
warm cozy blankets
and snuggly galore

i can breathe in here
it never feels alone
for the first time
in a long time
i feel like
i'm home

falling

15

unwavering she feels
the scissor tips sharp razer edge
floating feather pieces falter as they
spin away from her

and he collides, lonesome glider
as the she icarus plummets into him
they kiss for a moment
and she forgets that she was falling

yeah,
she forgets that she was falling

something

something in your eyes

sugar in your smile

when I look at you

i just hope you'll stay awhile

beside you

things seem a little brighter

i laugh a little more

my load feels a little lighter

Everglow

You broke the shadow
Without fight
Chased it away with
Tender light

Still warm
Still flickering
I hold you still with me,
Perennial flame
Everlasting candlelight

Jonah

you are warm
like summer sun rays
dancing on my skin
chlorophylls sunkissed dream
pushing up little freckled saplings
whenever you grin

sweet like wildflower honey
stirred in with a little gin
when you're around
my friends think i'm intoxicated but
you just make my heart spin

Walking On Stars

I'm walking on stars
Teetering forward
Pathway thrown off
By the presence of your gravity
Sat far too long
Complacent in a single place
Lonely little planet
Floating by itself in space
Stepping onto static
Following a trail of stardust
All the way to your coordinates

I'm walking on stars
Laughing all along the way
Holding onto my foot
Thrown off axis
I begin to sway
Pulled into your orbit
You catch me in a milky way
I'm grasped by the freckles of your galaxies
Gazing into two burnt sienna infinities
I can hardly voice the complexities
Of the universe I behold before me

I'm walking on stars

Our fingers intertwine a constellation
Baby you've got me caught in parallax
As I drift in synodic space
Towards you
And away from aphelion
With you I am a reoccurring supernova
With each passing lunar phase
Our luminance together
My love for you feels astral
Amongst the cosmos
Interstellar

we

i rather like
the me

that i get to be

whenever
you and i

become we

Thank You

Requited
tears
.
Flowing
heart
;
Embrace,
endear.
Gentle drumming start
;
Love and life
in my ear.
I can only
Pray
;
One Day
Together
We'll be
Counting
The
Years

The Underside

That side of you dear
The one that may cry
The one that says sorry
And explains to me why
The one that feels lost
And doesn't have the words to describe
The millions of feelings
That you might feel inside
That side that feels lonely
Amongst a crowded room
Everyone you love is a stranger
May as well just hide
Where you might struggle
Though you wish to coincide
That side that feels trapped
And just wants to collide
The side that you might fear
That side of you dear
It can be beautiful
To me this is clear
Don't lose this side of you
Keep it close, near
Your soft tender heart
Love it to tears,
Tend to its scars

Help it survive
One day soon
Lest you stay kind
That little side of you
May even start to thrive